In His Foo

30 Days with a Great Spiritual Teacher

In His Footsteps

∎ ∎ ∎ ∎ ∎ ∎ ∎ ∎ ∎ ∎ ∎ ∎ ∎

Living Prayer, Poverty, and Peace with

FRANCIS OF ASSISI

JOHN KIRVAN

ave maria press AmP **Notre Dame, Indiana**

JOHN KIRVAN, who conceived this series and has authored most of its titles, writes primarily about classical spirituality. His other recent books include *God Hunger, Raw Faith, Silent Hope,* and *There Is A God, There Is No God.*

The morning meditation passages have been freely adapted into contemporary English from the three volumes of *Early Documents of Francis of Assisi* (published by the Franciscan Institute of St. Bonaventure University, St. Bonaventure, NY), from *Francis and Clare, Complete Works* (Classics of Western Spirituality, © 1982 by Paulist Press Inc.), and from *Bonaventure, The Soul's Journey into God* (Classics of Western Spirituality, © 1978 by Paulist Press Inc.).

www.avemariapress.com
International Standard Book Number: 1-59471-027-9
Cover and text design by Katherine Robinson Coleman
Printed and bound in the United States of America.

Library of Congress Cataloging-in-Publication Data
Kirvan, John J.
  In his footsteps : living prayer, poverty, and peace with Francis of Assisi / John Kirvan.
      p. cm. -- (Thirty days with a great spiritual teacher)
  Includes bibliographical references and index.
  ISBN 1-59471-027-9 (pbk. : alk. paper)
  1. Francis, of Assisi, Saint, 1182-1226--Meditations. 2. Catholic Church--Prayer-books and devotions--English.
I. Francis, of Assisi, Saint, 1182-1226. II. Title. III. Series: 30 days with a great spiritual teacher.

  BX4700.F6K57 2005
  242'.2--dc22

                                    2005010288

Contents

THE BLESSING FOR BROTHER LEO

May the Lord bless you and keep you.
May he show his face to you and be merciful to you.
May he turn his countenance to you and give you peace.
May the Lord bless you Brother Leo.

—FRANCIS OF ASSISI

Francis of Assisi

Francis of Assisi (1181/82–1226) was a quiet, almost silent man. We don't know for certain whether he actually left any writings behind, and it is even questionable that he wrote the great prayers attached to his name.

But his way of life delivered a spiritual message more powerful than any he might have spoken or written, a message that for more than twelve centuries has shaped our life with God and each other.

This quiet man, by his simple, life-shattering act of stripping himself of all his possessions and putting poverty at the center of his life, turned history's notion of spirituality upside down.

Our life with God, he reminded us, is inextricably bound to poverty, not to some romantic version of poverty, not to some metaphoric poverty, but to the raw, unforgiving poverty of the poor—the poverty of the streets, the poverty of hunger, the poverty of homelessness.

We have arrived at that moment when we realize that if we are going to take Francis seriously—which means taking God seriously—we will have to take poverty seriously.

This book is about that moment.

It is a very discomforting moment.

At first glance no saint seems more available, less threatening, more comfortable to be with than Francis of Assisi. He is, after all, the same serene figure who graces the garden. He is the same gentle saint who talks with the animals.

But now Francis is talking poverty. He is saying that either we embrace a life of prayer and poverty or we miss the whole point of what he has to say to us. We will miss the peace God promises us.

It is a very discomforting moment.

Francis reveals himself as a very disconcerting saint.

Customs to the contrary, he is not an easy saint to understand. He resists first impressions.

He enchants us even as he leads us along demanding paths.

It is not easy to walk in his footsteps, but it can be done.

If we are to take Francis seriously—if we are to take ourselves seriously—we will have to rescue him from the warm fuzzies in which we and our culture have tried over the centuries to imprison him.

Almost from that day in the town center when Francis cast aside everything he possessed, there has been a steady stream of men and women anxious to live as he lived. Anxious to pray as Francis prayed. Anxious to cut their way through the sentiments and myths to the life of prayer that Francis promised would lead to the peace of God.

Bonaventure did it.

Clare did it.

And so have tens of thousands of others.

So too can we.

How to Pray This Book

The purpose of this book is to open a gate for you, to make accessible the spiritual experience and wisdom of one of history's most important spiritual teachers, Francis of Assisi, and those who followed in his footsteps.

This is not a book for mere reading. It invites you to meditate and pray its words on a daily basis over a period of thirty days.

It is a handbook for a spiritual journey.

Before you read the "rules" for taking this spiritual journey, remember that this book is meant to free your spirit, not to confine it. If on any day the meditation does not resonate well with you, turn elsewhere to find a passage which seems best to fit the spirit of your day and your soul. Don't hesitate to repeat a day as often as you like until you feel that you have discovered what the Spirit, through the words of the author, has to say to your spirit.

Here are suggestions for one way to use this book as a cornerstone of your prayers.

As Your Day Begins

As the day begins set aside a quiet moment in a quiet place to read the meditation suggested for the day.

This passage is short. It never runs more than a couple of hundred words, but it has been carefully selected to give a spiritual focus, a spiritual center to your whole day. It is designed to remind you, as another day begins, of your own existence at a spiritual level. It is meant to put you in the presence of the spiritual master who is your companion and teacher on this journey. But most of all, the purpose of this passage is to remind you that at this moment and at every moment during the day, you will be living and acting in the presence of a God who invites you continually, but quietly, to live in and through him.

A word of advice: Read slowly. Very slowly. The meditation has been broken down into sense lines to help you do just this. Don't read to get to the end, but savor each part of the meditation. You never know what short phrase or word will trigger a response in your spirit. Give the words a chance. After all, you are not just reading this passage, you are praying it. You are establishing a mood of serenity for your whole day. What's the rush?

All Through Your Day

Immediately following the day's reading, you will find a single sentence which we call a mantra, a word borrowed from the Hindu tradition. This phrase is meant as a companion for your spirit as it moves through a busy day. Write it down on a 3" x 5" card or on the appropriate page of your daybook. Look at it as often as you can. Repeat it quietly to yourself and go on your way.

It is not meant to stop you in your tracks or to distract you from your responsibilities but simply and gently to remind you of the presence of God and your desire to respond to this presence.

As Your Day Is Ending

This is a time for letting go of the day.

Find a quiet place and quiet your spirit. Breathe deeply. Inhale, exhale—slowly and deliberately, again and again, until you feel your body let go of its tension.

Now read the evening prayer slowly, phrase by phrase. You may recognize at once that we have taken one of the most familiar evening prayers of the Christian tradition and woven into it both phrases taken from the meditation with which you began your day and the mantra that has accompanied you all through your day. In this way, a simple evening prayer gathers together the spiritual character of the day that is now ending as it began—in the presence of God.

It is a time for summary and closure.

Invite God to embrace you with love and to protect you through the night.

Sleep well.

Some Other Ways to Use This Book

1. Use it any way your spirit suggests. As mentioned earlier, skip a passage that doesn't resonate with you on a given day, or repeat for a second day or even several days a passage if its richness speaks to you. The truths of a spiritual life are not absorbed in a day, or for that matter, in a lifetime. So take your time. Be patient with the Lord. Be patient with yourself.

2. Take two passages and/or their mantras—the more contrasting the better—and "bang" them together. Spend time discovering how their similarities or differences illumine your path.

3. Start a spiritual journal to record and deepen your experience

of this thirty-day journey. Using either the mantra or another phrase from the reading that appeals to you, write a spiritual account of your day, a spiritual reflection. Create your own meditation.

4. Join millions who are seeking to deepen their spiritual life by uniting with others to form a small group. More and more people are doing this to support each other in their mutual quest. Meet once a week, or at least every other week, to discuss and pray about one of the meditations. There are many books and guides available to help you make such a group effective.

Prayer

He surrendered his whole self
to the presence of God.

He would petition his father,
talk with his friend,
and be joyful with his spouse.

He sought not to pray,
but to become a prayer.

—THOMAS OF CELANO, C. 1229

Day One

∎

My Day Begins

His biographer would say of Francis:
"His first haven was prayer.
And it did not last for a mere moment,
but for as long as possible."

Francis knew
that our journey to the peace of God
is a journey of prayer,
and that without prayer,
without complete dependence on God,

the yearning for peace
that aches in our soul
will take us nowhere.

Without prayer,
our most persistent efforts
are pointless.

They go nowhere.

But divine aid
is ours for the asking.

God gives his peace
to anyone who seeks it
with a humble heart.

To anyone, that is, who prays.

To anyone, that is, who is willing
to accept peace as a gift
that cannot be earned.

To anyone who desires the peace of God
with his whole heart and soul,
but who knows
and accepts
that desire is not enough.

Our desire,
our good will,
must lead to prayer,
because only prayer
can lead to peace.

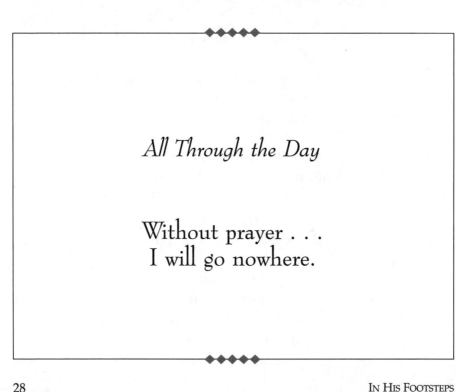

All Through the Day

Without prayer . . .
I will go nowhere.

My Day Is Ending

In the dark silence
of this night
I reach out to you in hope,
in prayer.

Grant me safe haven.

Grant me that peace
which surpasses all understanding,
that peace
which I desire
more than anything else,
that peace for which I pray,
but which only you can give.

Grant me patience.

I am completely dependent on you.

I know that without you
the desire for peace
that fills my soul
will go nowhere,
can go nowhere.

Here in the quiet of this night
hear my prayers.

In the dark silence of this night
grant me safe haven.

Day Two

My Day Begins

The great Franciscan theologian,
St. Bonaventure,
cautions us against
expecting to find God
in the clarity of theology
and study.

God is not
where we most expect to find him.

God is found
not in understanding,
but in prayer,
not in the strengths of our humanity,
but in mystery,
in the enveloping fire
that is his presence.

If we want to know more
about the journey into peace,
we must go from light into darkness,
from knowing to not knowing,
from the cares of our day
to a silenced heart,
from this world
to the world of our Father.

Then it will be enough,
but only then.
"We will have looked to grace,
not to doctrine,
to desire,
not to understanding,"
Bonaventure wrote.

"To the cry of prayer,
not to the labor of study."

Only then will we be able to say,
You are the God of my heart,
the God who is my portion
for eternity.

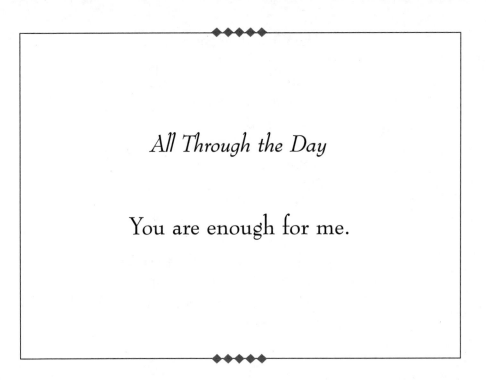

All Through the Day

You are enough for me.

My Day Is Ending

Here in the quiet of this night
I reach out
for that peace
which surpasses all understanding,
for that peace
which I desire
more than anything else,
but which only you can give.

Let me be content,
as I wait for your peace,
to live with your mystery,
content not to know
what I cannot know.

Let it be enough.

Let it take me
where my words are not needed,
where only a silent prayer
can light up the darkness.

Take me with you
into the wordless night.
Answer my prayers
with a taste of that peace
that surpasses all my imaginings.
That peace which I desire,
but which only you can give.

Day Three

My Day Begins

St. Bonaventure reminds us that
as complicated and mysterious
as it may seem at times,
there is no great secret to the search for God.

"Wherever we are, God is."

Francis knew well and profoundly
that God shines forth in all of creation.
God is where we are, wherever we are.

We are where God is.
Always.

But like Francis, we need
to listen to creation.
We need to open our eyes,
and keep them open, to the world God has given us.

If we listen,
if we open our heart,
we will discover that God is here
to be seen and heard.

Traces of God can be found
wherever we look,
wherever we listen,

wherever we walk,
wherever we are.

But we have to make a choice.

We can choose to live
blind to his splendor,
deaf to his voice,
speechless in his presence.

Or we may choose
to see, hear, praise, love,
worship, glorify, and honor
the God who is alive in all creatures.

We can choose to pray.

All Through the Day

God is here.

My Day Is Ending

Here in the dark silence
of this night
I reach out in prayer
for that peace
which surpasses all understanding,
for that peace
which I desire
more than anything else,
but which only you can give.

Remind me that here
in the dark silence
of this night
I will not need words.

But I will need to listen
for your presence.

And if I am to see you
in your creation,
I will need
to keep the eyes of my soul open
even in the dark.

Even in the darkest night,
even in its deepest silence,
let me see,
hear, praise, love,
worship, glorify,
and honor you
in all of your creation.

Don't let me settle
for anything less.

Day Four

My Day Begins

When Francis sought out
the isolation of the mountains,
which was frequently,
he knew exactly what he was looking for.
He wanted, he needed, a place to pray.

So do we!
We need to follow him
into silence.

We need to spend time with him,
beyond the limits of our imagination,
beyond what we can understand.

We need to spend time conscious of God.

And we need to spend time
alive to the mystery
of who we are.

We are creatures created in the likeness of God.

But that's only half our story.

We are a forgetful people,
constantly needing to be reminded of who we are.

We need to remember that
God has taken on the likeness of our humanity.
God has become visible as a human being

so that we might see him
and love him.
So that we do not forget who we are.
Who God is.

We are a people who need to pray,
who need, that is, to recall
who we are
and how close to our creator
we are as we live our lives.

We are a people who,
in both the silent and busy corners of our life,
must remember to pray.

We are a people
who need to join Francis in mountain isolation.

We need to pray lest we forget.

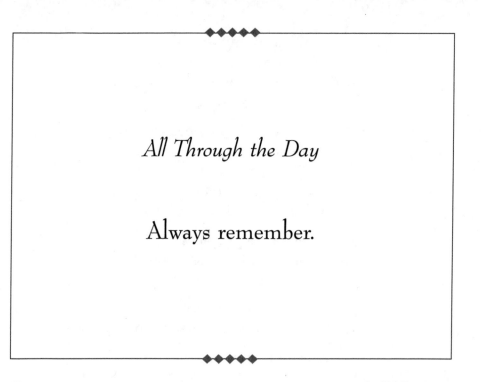

All Through the Day

Always remember.

My Day Is Ending

Here in the dark silence
of this night
hear my prayer
for that peace
which surpasses all understanding,
for that peace
which I desire
more than anything else,
but which only you can give.

I need to spend time with you
beyond the limits of my imagination,
beyond what I can understand.

I need to remember that
you have taken on the likeness of our humanity.

You have become a visible human being
so that I might see you,
and love you,
and not forget
who I am.

And lest I forget,
I need to pray.
I need to recall
who I am
and how close you are.

I need to seek you out
not just in the silence of your mountain,
But in the busiest
corner of my day,
and here
in the darkest hour of this night.

Day Five

My Day Begins

There are familiar paths
for the spiritual traveler
and paths that are easy on the soul,
but neither of these is the path of Francis
and his followers.

Left to ourselves
we would place all our hope
in earnest study,
understanding, and knowledge.

We need Bonaventure
to remind us that
they are not enough.

"Mere reading will not be enough
to assure the peace of God."

In his great work,
The Soul's Journey Into God,
Bonaventure reminds us that
our journey into the peace of God
is a journey that can succeed
only in the company of God.

It is a journey of wonder,
of piety,
of love and humility.
It is above all
a journey that can be traveled

only when divinely graced
by the God whose peace we seek.

It is, above all,
a journey we cannot take alone.

It is a hard realization.

But this is the road,
the only road,
by which we arrive at the peace of God,
the peace that we so desperately seek
but which only God can provide.

This is the peace
proclaimed and given to us
by our Lord Jesus Christ
and preached again and again
by our father Francis.

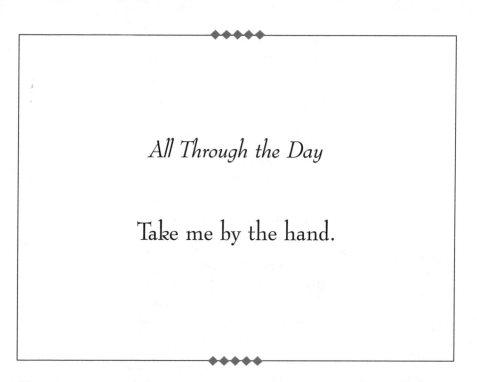

All Through the Day

Take me by the hand.

My Day Is Ending

Here in the dark silence
of this night
hear my prayer, Lord,
for that peace
which surpasses all understanding.

In this dark silence,
with your grace
as my strength and courage,
and Francis
as my guide,
I can leave
the safe path
I always have chosen.

Instead, I can
travel with you
on a journey of wonder,

of piety,
of love, and humility.

In this journey
I know that
I am not alone.

Take me by the hand, Francis,
along the only road
that leads to the peace I seek.

Show me, Francis,
The path you took.

Take me by the hand
along this road to peace.
That has been
proclaimed and given to us
by our Lord Jesus Christ,
and preached again and again
by you, my brother, Francis.

Day Six

My Day Begins

As Clare once reminded her sisters,
we are called
to embrace a broken Christ.
He was
more beautiful than all of God's creatures,
but for our sake
he became the lowliest of all,
despised, wounded, and broken for us.

When we pray,
we pray to that broken Christ.

We are drawn
inevitably, however unwittingly,
into worlds we never expected, never wanted to inhabit.
We are drawn to
the broken world of Christ,
our broken world.

Our prayers take us
where we never expected to go,
into lands
where, in truth, we would prefer not to go.
We expected to find a beautiful God,
a consoling God.
But we find ourselves instead
in the company of a broken Christ.

To our surprise,
we find ourselves in a land

of disappointment and challenge.
This is not the surprise we expected.
This is the God who for our sake
became the lowliest of all,
despised, wounded, and broken for us.

This is the God
who answers our prayers,
who is the answer to our prayers.

We know
that only if we suffer with him now,
only if we weep with him now,
can we share the joy
that he has promised us.

Only if we share his brokenness
can we share the wholeness that we seek,
which he has promised.

All Through the Day

Our Christ is a broken Christ.

My Day Is Ending

Here in the dark silence
of this night
hear my prayer, Lord,
for that peace
which surpasses all understanding.

I do not know what to expect
in the darkness of this night.

I have been told that, for our sake,
you have become one of us.
Instead of a beautiful God,
a consoling God,
I should find myself
in the company of a broken Christ.

In this dark silence
I must expect
not a Christ more beautiful
than all the children of humankind,
but a Christ who, for our sake,
for my sake,
has become like the lowliest of all people,
someone who shares my broken humanity,
someone like me . . .
who enters this dark night
despised, wounded, and broken.

For me.

Someone who will answer my prayers,
someone who is the answer to my prayers:
a broken Christ
to console my broken soul.

Day Seven

My Day Begins

Many, if not most of us,
exist on the surface of our lives.
We are
oblivious to the incomparable spiritual treasures
at the heart of our being,
oblivious to the liberating, expansive mysteries
that wait to be unearthed,
explored, and embraced,
oblivious to the mysteries that promise us
a new life.

We are content,
as often as not,
to travel the convenient and familiar ways,
content to trade the challenging mystery of God's presence
for a familiar life of comfort.
But Clare is here to remind us that
until we uncover and discover
the treasures that lie at the heart of our being,
we are destined
to live only half alive.

She is here to remind us that
we become fully alive
only when we leave behind familiar paths,
only when we go beyond our imagination,
only when we surrender the life we live
for the life that might be.

We become fully alive
only when we surrender
to the incomparable treasures
that still lie buried within our soul.

We become fully alive
only when the mystery of God is
no longer buried, but celebrated.

We go on living
only when we recognize
that we are in the presence of God.

We become fully alive
only when we pray.

All Through the Day

Let me pray.

My Day Is Ending

Here in the dark silence
of this night,
hear my prayer, Lord,
for that peace
which surpasses all understanding.

It is a peace that will escape me
as long as I live where I am now,
skating on the surface of my soul,
hiding from the incomparable spiritual treasures
that are buried there.

It is no way to live.
It is no way to find the peace
that I so glibly claim
over and over again
to be seeking.

This peace I seek
is not for those who settle
for easy, familiar words,
those like me
who are content
to travel convenient and familiar paths,
who are content
to trade the challenging mystery of God's presence
for a life of comfort.
This much I do know.

This peace I seek
will escape me
until I learn to pray,
until in the darkness of a night like this
I surrender to the sacred treasures
that lie buried within me.

Day Eight

My Day Begins

It is easy, much too easy,
to pursue sacred knowledge
but in the process
lose sight of prayer.

Prayer is the whole point.

But since, from our earliest years,
we are taught to identify prayer with words,
we come to believe that
it is the words that matter.

But they don't.

Perhaps too, it is because
we put rafts of theology into our pursuit of God,
we come to believe that
our spiritual success depends on
how much we know.

But it doesn't.

Our efforts,
no matter how profound and persistent,
are not what matter.
They can, in fact, become
an ongoing temptation to abandon prayer
in favor of our own efforts.

What matters is recognizing
the presence of God in our lives
and opening ourselves to her,
our soul emptied of
words and images,
that can never be
more than our own creation,
free of everything that is not God.

What matters is our learning
how to pray,
learning how to go without words,
when words fill our heart,
learning to live silently with God
as God loves silently with us.

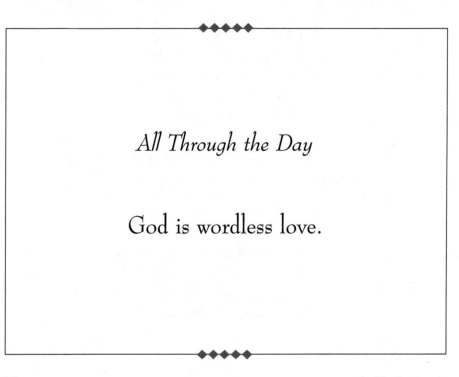

All Through the Day

God is wordless love.

My Day Is Ending

Here in the dark silence
of this night
hear my prayer, Lord,
for that peace
which surpasses all understanding.

Hear my stuttering prayers.
I know the words I use,
which I am so dependent on,
may not be what is most important.

But as this day ends
I find myself uneasy
because I am speechless.

I find myself fishing in the dark
for something to say to you,
for something to say to myself.
I find myself
seeking out words
to fill the silence,
seeking out words
when it is only you
who can fill the void I feel.

But here in the dark
I pray the best I can.

I will look
not for words,
but for your silent presence.

Hear my prayer.

Day Nine

My Day Begins

In all the words written about Francis
(and there have been millions),
in all the stories and anecdotes
that surround his life,
nothing captures the heart of Francis
better than his biographer's insight:

"He sought not just to pray,
but to become prayer,
to live in such a way
as to define prayer."

He wrote of Francis' life with God
that prayer was not a skill,
not a practice,
not something he did.
It was something he became.

He replaced words with his life.

Prayer became his identity.
It was who he was.

And here is the point:
It is who,
it is what,
we are to become.

Bit by bit we are
to become, as Francis became,
not just prayerful,

but a prayer.
We are to pray in such a way
as to define our life,
to live in such a way
as to be a prayer.

It will not be easy.

After a lifetime of searching for the right word,
it will not be easy
to put words in their proper place,
not easy to let prayer become
our identity.

It will not be easy
to replace our words
with our life.

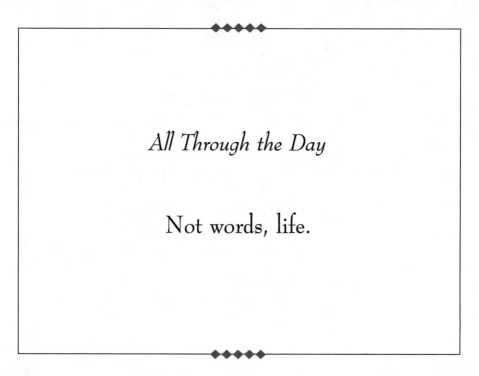

All Through the Day

Not words, life.

My Day Is Ending

Here in the dark silence
of this night
hear my prayer, Lord,
for that peace
which surpasses all understanding.

Hear too, Lord, my silence.

For even as I search the night
for words that I might bring to you,
for words to capture
the desires of my soul,
I fall silent.

Hear my silence.
For it is who I am.
It is all that I am.

I am my silence.
I am my prayer.

Hear me.

With Francis at my side,
show me how, bit by bit,
to become as he became
not just prayerful,
but a prayer.

Teach me to pray as he prayed.

Teach me to live as he lived,
in such a way as to be a prayer.

Hear that prayer.

Hear me.

Day Ten

My Day Begins

As at so many other moments
when we have stopped
to meditate on the life of Francis,
we can be overly quick
to see something romantic,
almost fantasy-like,
in the story of his frequent return
to a favorite retreat,
a hermitage where he could give himself
more fully to prayerful contemplation.

At that moment
we would readily wrap ourselves in silence
and join Francis in his hermitage,
quite certain that alone with God
we could—we would—
give ourselves over to contemplation.

But there is something that
in our fantasizing we easily, frequently, forget.

Francis journeyed to his retreat
weak from the heat
of a hot summer day.

We forget that
even Francis reaches his place of prayer
only after

a long and steep climb,
only after tending to the needs
of the poor.

No one travels alone.
Not Francis,
not us.

We enter the retreat we seek,
we enter our place of prayer
in the company of others.

In the end there is no seclusion.

There is only God,
and our fellow travelers.

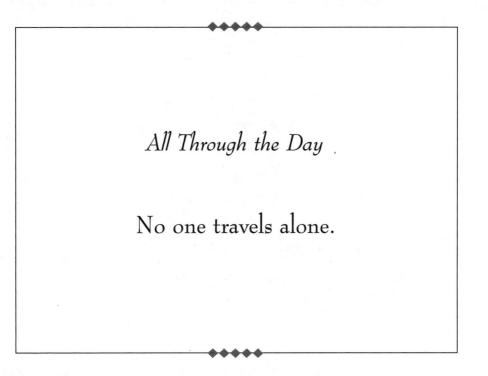

All Through the Day

No one travels alone.

My Day Is Ending

Here in the dark silence
of this night
hear my prayer, Lord,
for that peace
which surpasses all understanding.

I want you to give me that peace.
I want you to make it easy to for me
to give myself over more fully to you,
to prayerful contemplation.

But that's not the way it is. Is it?

It wasn't easy for Francis.
It won't be easy for me.

I know the path will be steep and long.
Here in this quiet darkness
let me take at least a first step.

Let me,
if just for a moment of silence,
if just for a corner of the night,
embrace
the silent darkness of this place,
of this night.

Let me
make of this place,
of this night,
a small hermitage
where I can find you,
where I can find myself,
where I can take a first step
on a long and steep climb.

Poverty

From the time of his conversion,
Francis gave himself
with all longing
to searching for, finding, and embracing Lady Poverty.

He never wavered, nor did he fear injury.
He never shrank from effort.
Nor did he shun bodily discomfort
in order to achieve his desire:
to reach her to whom
the Lord
had entrusted
the keys of the kingdom of heaven.

Day Eleven

My Day Begins

There is more than one kind of poverty.

There is a root, physical poverty
that in our age of affluence
is a scourge and a spiritual scandal.

This is the poverty
that is daily thrust upon millions
who go hungry and homeless.

This is the poverty
of suffering that populates our TV screens,
our politics, and our spirituality.

It is a poverty that
digs into our consciousness,
a poverty that
demands our practical response
unless we are prepared
to call our spirituality by what would be
its proper name—"a sham."

It is a poverty that demands
more than our prayers.

The hungry must be fed,
their bodies must be clothed,
their families must be sheltered.

It has always been thus,
but in our times
we cannot claim to be ignorant.

The impoverished millions
reach out of the nightly news
to insist on our attention.

We cannot claim
to be without means.
Our lands are abundant with
what others lack.

Most importantly,
the Lord has spoken
through our brother Francis,
whose way we have chosen.

We must listen.

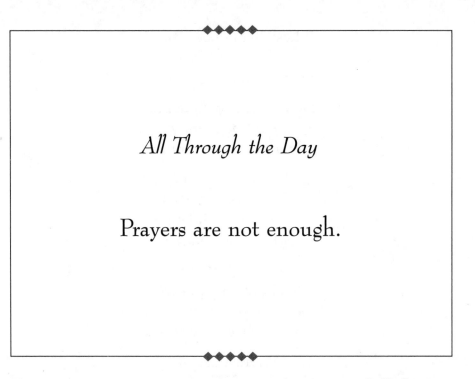

All Through the Day

Prayers are not enough.

My Day Is Ending

Even as this day ends,
I know that in truth
I'm not ready for poverty,
not ready to be poor,
not yet ready
to walk in your footsteps
or in the footsteps of the poor
and the homeless,
not ready for true poverty.

But here in the silent darkness of this night
I dare not deafen myself
to those who are truly poor,

to those whose need
for food in their bellies is real.

It is not enough
just to pray for them,
to remember them only in my prayer book.
In the streets across the world,
and in my neighborhood,
the hungry must be fed,
their bodies must be clothed,
their families must be sheltered.

And I must not
let my soul sleep
as long as
I can hear the voices of the poor.

Day Twelve

My Day Begins

There is more than one kind of poverty.

Beyond the imposed poverty
of the hungry and the homeless
there is the chosen poverty of Francis.

When Francis was still very young
there came a time for him
to put aside all the possessions

that had, up to that moment,
dominated his life.

He sold everything he had,
even the horse he was riding.
He recentered his whole being
around his decision to live in poverty.

His life defined
a radically simple
and demanding spirituality
that was right
not only for his own life and century,
but in a special way
for our affluent times.

To choose poverty
is to choose God.

To choose God
is to choose poverty.

God and poverty
have always been inextricably bound together.

But in our age of affluence,
when to a smothering degree
we have become what we possess,
the connection becomes central
to our relationship with God.

Others might define their spiritual life
in terms of prayer.

But Francis was clear and adamant:
Spirituality is about being poor.

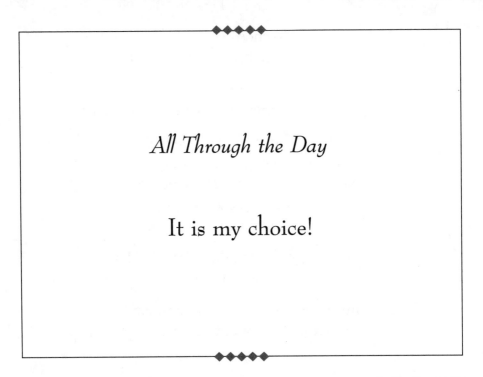

All Through the Day

It is my choice!

My Day Is Ending

Even as this day ends,
I know that in truth
I'm not ready for poverty,
not ready to be poor,
not yet ready
to walk in your footsteps
or in the footsteps of the poor
and the homeless,
not ready for true poverty.

I am not yet ready to believe
that to truly love God
I must become poor.

But here in the silent darkness of this night
I can hear the voice of Francis,
reminding me

how far I have yet to go,
how much stands in my way,
how many things I am attached to,
how much I couldn't possibly do without.

But sooner or later
all those things that I now "need,"
that I can't "do without,"
must make room for God.

Poverty is a lot to ask,
a lot to choose.

It is a choice that is never easy.

But it can be done.
Francis did it.

Francis chose to be poor.
And so, in the end, must we.

Day Thirteen

■

My Day Begins

There is more than one kind of poverty.

There is a kind of poverty
that permeates every corner of our lives,
an atmosphere
that our soul breathes,
an attitude of the spirit that
passes judgment on all our choices
both great and small.

It is a judgment
passed by our lives

on our lives,
a consistent, all embracing judgment.

It is a universal poverty
that requires us,
in the face of
every character-forming moment,
to ask ourselves:
Does this choice free me from things
or deepen my slavery?

It is either
one or the other.

"No servant can be
the slave of two masters" (Mt 6:24).

Either I will hate one
and love the other,
or I will be devoted to the first

and think nothing of the second.
I cannot serve God and things.

This poverty of spirit
is the inescapable
measurement of our soul.

It is the way of Francis,
for whom poverty of spirit
was not just a question of ridding himself
of all his possessions.

It was a way
for him to define life with God,
as it will be for us.

It was a way
of recentering, in God,
his very being.

All Through the Day

Poverty is the measure of my soul.

My Day Is Ending

Even as this day ends,
I know that in truth
I'm not ready for poverty,
not ready to be poor,
not yet ready
to walk in your footsteps
or in the footsteps of the poor
and the homeless,
not ready for true poverty.

I am not yet ready
to accept that truly loving you
is not a sometime thing,
but a fundamental choice
that permeates every part of my life.
It is a choice that affects every other choice.

It leaves nothing untouched.

When I choose you
I choose Lady Poverty.

I tell myself that I cannot be
the servant of two masters;

I tell myself that I cannot
serve God and money.

But here in the quiet honesty of this night
I know that I will go on trying to be poor,
even as I go on deepening my slavery to things.

But now and then with your strength
I will choose you,
at least for the moment.

Day Fourteen

■

My Day Begins

Many, if not most of us,
cherish a quiet hope
that there is,
there must be,
some other way,
some other path,
that leads
to the kingdom of heaven,
that bypasses being poor,

that bypasses
doing without.

As it is,
over the years
the poverty that we honor in our prayers
has often been
reduced to a soul-comforting metaphor.

But for Francis,
poverty was not a figure of speech.
Nor should it be for us.

It is a raw, grinding reality.
And as long as our poverty
is no more than a spiritual
stand-in for being poor,
we have missed the point.

Poverty grounds us
like no other element
of our spiritual journey
in ragged-edged reality.

We are not talking poetry.

Either our lives are thing-driven
or they are not.

Until we go without
we will never understand
what drove Francis—
barefooted,
ragged,
and joyful.

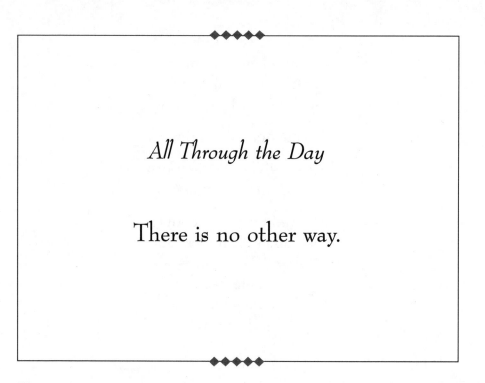

All Through the Day

There is no other way.

My Day Is Ending

Even as this day ends,
I know that in truth
I'm not ready for poverty,
not ready to be poor,
not yet ready
to walk in the footsteps of Francis,
or in the footsteps of the poor
and the homeless,
not ready for true poverty.

I need him more than ever
to lead me
through the dark silence of this night,
to where you wait for me.

I know that I will waver
as Francis never did.
I will be afraid,
and I will shrink
from the demands of the journey.
I will stumble along the way.

But with the courage of Francis
planted in my heart,
I will reach into
the dark silence of this night
and find his Lady Poverty,
she to whom
the Lord has entrusted
the keys to
the kingdom of the poor.

Day Fifteen

My Day Begins

Spend even a few minutes
in the presence of Francis
and some things become very clear.

There is in Francis
a singleness of heart
that we must recognize
if we are to understand
the spirituality of this remarkable man,
if he is to become our teacher.

At the center of his heart
is a commitment to poverty.

Asked for a description of his life,
he might say:

'I am a simple man.
I am a poor man.
Once I decided to follow Jesus
it never occurred to me
that I could do anything else.
It never occurred to me
that I could be any other kind of man,
that I could be anything else
but poor.'

There is something else
about his poverty
we must know.

For him,
poverty was a way of life.

It was not a sociological fact.

It was not a virtue
or a spiritual practice.

It was a
life-shaping choice.

The choice is ours to make.

With Francis,
we can choose to be poor.

With him, we can
choose poverty
for the sake of others.

All Through the Day

Choose poverty.

My Day Is Ending

Even as this day ends,
I know that in truth
I'm not ready for poverty,
not ready to be poor,
not yet ready
to walk in your footsteps.

My soul wants too many things.
I depend on them.
I am afraid to be without them.

I am afraid to have only you.

But here in the darkness of this silent night,
if just for a moment,

give me the courage
to be alone with you.

For this moment
let me close my ears
to the thousand voices
that have filled my day
with promises that still tug at my soul.

For this moment
close my ears to every voice
but yours.

You have said that you are enough.
In the silence of this night
I need to believe you.

I believe.

Day Sixteen

My Day Begins

We are urged
to be clear about the path
we have chosen to walk,
about the gate
through which we have chosen
to enter into life.

But it is hard to trace the path
walked by Francis.
For millions, over centuries,
it has been reduced
to a garden path.

For many,
Francis was—is—not much more
than a pretty ornament.

We need to learn
that his way is not
one of summer garden indolence,
of shaded monastic paths,
of perfectly tailored religious habits,
a tamed bird in hand.

His path makes demands
that cut to our very soul,
that shape our very lives.

He demands that we embrace poverty.
Not metaphorical poverty,
but raw, abrasive poverty.

Poverty that costs.

He demands
that we choose to be poor
as he was poor.

Our task is
to cut through the spiritual clutter
of the world
and of our lives,
to reach the path that
he lived and walked,
and then to walk in his footsteps
making poverty the center of our being.

Our task is
to make poverty
the gate
through which
we can enter into life.

About these things,
difficult as they are,
we need to be very clear.

All Through the Day

The gate is narrow.

My Day Is Ending

Even as this day ends,
I know that in truth
I'm not ready for poverty,
not ready to be poor,
not yet ready
to walk in your footsteps,
or in the footsteps of the poor
and the homeless,
not ready for true poverty.

Still, here in this night,
I summon up what little courage I have
to cut through the clutter of my soul,

to find the path that you walked,
and to pass with you through its narrow gate.

I have no choice.
Like you, I must walk
in the footsteps of the poor,
choosing poverty,
and as you did,
making it the center of my being.

However unready my soul may be,
If I am to find life
I must pass this way.

I must walk the path you walked
and pass through its narrow gate.
It is a choice I must make.

Day Seventeen

My Day Begins

For Francis
poverty was a lady, his lady.

Not a discreet lady,
careful not to embarrass anyone.

Not a model of security,
not a financial planner.

She was—*she is*—Lady Poverty,
as in poor,
as in the enemy of greed.

She allows for no hiding places.
She knows
no softening figures of speech.

Her poverty is
not a metaphor.
It is not a symbol.

It is the hard edged reality
of the poor.

She is called Lady Poverty
and she means
to be taken at her word.

She calls us to be poor,
to abandon
our attachment to things.

She calls us to be
as she is,
as the poor of the streets are,
the companions of Francis—
the poor man,
the *"poverello."*

Like Francis,
like Lady Poverty,
like the poor of the streets,
our reliance is on God.

There is nothing else.
There is no one else.
We are the poor.

All Through the Day

I am the poor.

My Day Is Ending

Even as this day ends,
I know that in truth
I'm not ready for poverty,
not ready to be poor,
not yet ready
to walk in your footsteps
or in the footsteps of the poor
and the homeless,
not ready for true poverty.

Lady Poverty,
I am not ready for you.

So, here in this night,
I look for hiding places,
for shelters from the storm
that comes from choosing you
as my bride.

You were Francis' choice.
You were his lady,
and you allowed him
no illusions.
I still have some.

But I want you to be my lady.
I am not Francis.
I am not a hero.
I am just another poor human
and you are my Lady.

Day Eighteen

My Day Begins

There is no doubt
that when we first hear Francis
and his Lady
calling us to poverty,
saying it is poverty or nothing,
it can be very threatening,
even overwhelming.

A part of our soul
looks for an exit.
There must be
some other way to be "spiritual,"

some other way to respond to God,
some other easier way.
This way,
the way of Francis,
can seem impossible.

This way is
much too hard,
too far beyond
our spiritual reach.

But there is no exit.
There is no other way.
Poverty, as lived by Francis,
is not some exotic, extremist way
that seeks out the spiritual.
It is,
as Francis' life
constantly reminds us,
the only way

to free ourselves from slavery
to the world.

It is the simple everyday life of a poor man.

Until we escape materialism's hold on our soul
we are kidding ourselves
about living a spiritual, God-centered life.

Francis isn't about to change his mind.
He stubbornly repeats his insistence
that we choose to be poor.

It is scary.

It goes far beyond
where our soul has ever been,
but it's possible.
Francis did it.
So can we.

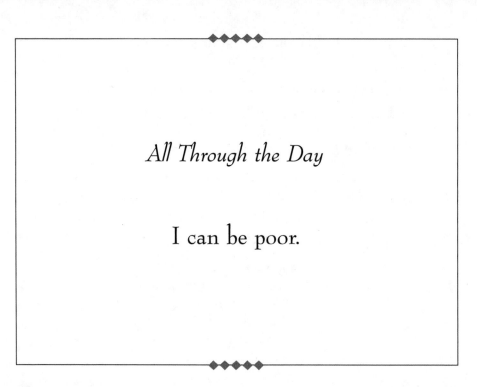

All Through the Day

I can be poor.

My Day Is Ending

Even as this day ends,
I know that in truth
I'm not ready for poverty,
not ready to be poor,
not yet ready
to walk in your footsteps
or in the footsteps of the poor
and the homeless,
not ready for true poverty.

In truth,
your way frightens me.
You are taking me too far beyond
where I am prepared to go.

But what is too far
and what is not far enough?

Given my druthers,
I would go only
as far as my comfort will take me.
This far, where I am now, but no farther.
But you are, I know, waiting for me,
just a step beyond my comfort.

A step into the darkness,
into a dark place where I have never been.

A place where slaves are freed.

A place where I could be free.

A place where you wait for me.

Day Nineteen

My Day Begins

There are no immediate rewards
for choosing poverty.

It's a hard road
that has no ending.

A hard road where no choice is final.

A road where each choice
is as demanding as the first.

A hard road where poverty must be chosen
again and again.

No one
knew this better than Clare,
whose commitment to poverty
matched Francis' depth and universality.

She never forgot
how hard the road can be,
how unrelenting is
the choice of poverty.

She had no illusions
about how rocky and hard
the road of poverty is,
how incredibly trying
it will be.

No matter the generosity of our soul,
no matter our determination;
our task is to stick with it.

Clare never left Francis' side,
never took back the promise she had made
to a life of poverty.

To us she says:
"Remember you are not alone.
Francis is with you.

I am with you.

The Lord is with you."

The true challenge of poverty
never changes.
It is to stay with it
to the end.

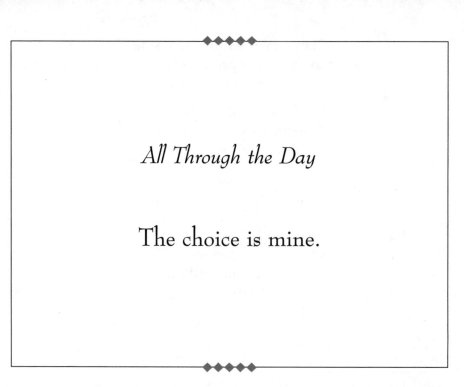

All Through the Day

The choice is mine.

My Day Is Ending

Even as this day ends,
I know that in truth
I'm not ready for poverty,
not ready to be poor,
not yet ready
to walk in your footsteps
or in the footsteps of the poor
and the homeless.

I am not yet ready
to believe that to truly love God
I must be poor.

But here in the silent darkness of this night
I know that in the end,
if I am to follow you,

I have no choice
but to be poor.

I know that for me it will be a lifelong journey
taken one step at a time.
It will be a lifetime of good intentions,

of promises made and broken,
of poverty embraced and abandoned.
I know that it will be about
stumbling and falling,
about finding my way
through days of good will and hope,
days filled with scratches and bruises,
days spent knowing that
your challenge of poverty will never change.

My task will be to stay with you
to the end.

Day Twenty

My Day Begins

Just how radical
the life and teaching of Francis is
becomes evident when we realize
that his response to the homeless,
to those who have no place to lay their head,
goes beyond building shelters.

You can almost hear him
responding to the challenge
laid down by the life of Jesus,

when faced with the actual
pain of the poor.

"I choose to live
as Jesus lived,
to have nowhere to rest my head,
to live shelterless."

"That," we can hear him say,
"is the way we are supposed to live."

There may be
something romantic
about the images of
the foxes with their dens,
and the birds of the air with their nests,
but there is nothing romantic
about being poor and shelterless.

The words of Jesus
drive home the gritty reality of poverty
and what it takes to embrace it
as a way of life.

To embrace it
as Francis embraced it.

To embrace it
as Jesus embraced it.

Lady Poverty
was his inseparable companion
throughout this journey.

She would be happy
to be ours.

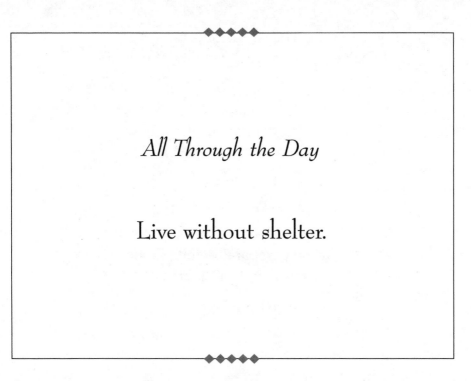

All Through the Day

Live without shelter.

My Day Is Ending

Even as this day ends,
I know that in truth
I'm not ready for poverty,
not ready to be poor,
not yet ready
to walk in your footsteps
or in the footsteps of the poor
and the homeless.

I am not yet ready
to believe that to truly love God
I must be poor.

But here in the silent darkness of this night
I am not sure how to respond.

I am not homeless,
but I live in a world of homelessness,
of whole families that are without a place
to lay their head.

It is easy for me to do nothing
and walk away,
because I cannot do enough.

But let me not at least do this:
Let me not fall asleep
undisturbed by the homeless
who this day and night
have sought to catch the attention of my soul.

Let me wake in the morning
with my soul right-side up.

Peace

In all his preaching,
before he set forth the word of God
to those gathered about,
Francis first prayed that they might have peace.
"The Lord give you peace," he would greet them.
For this reason many who had hated peace,
with the help of the Lord
embraced peace with all their heart
and were made children of peace.

—THOMAS OF CELANO, C. 1229

Day Twenty-One

My Day Begins

Like many young men
Francis grew up loving war.

For such young men war was
a romantic fantasy
that would lead them to adventure.
But it could also lead them to real war.

They, Francis included,
had to learn how to love peace.

So do we.

Our times have again
taught us that
the love of peace
does not come easily or naturally
to the human heart.

Peace is something that
we must learn to love,
and achieve at whatever cost.

Like Francis,
we are called
not just to be at peace,
but to be peacemakers.

We are called to be
instruments of peace.

No matter what effort,
no matter what suffering it may require,
we are called, like Francis,
to preserve peace of spirit and body
out of love for our Lord Jesus Christ.

Where there is suffering
we are called to make peace.

But it is only
with the help of the Lord
that we can embrace peace
with all our hearts
and become
children of peace.

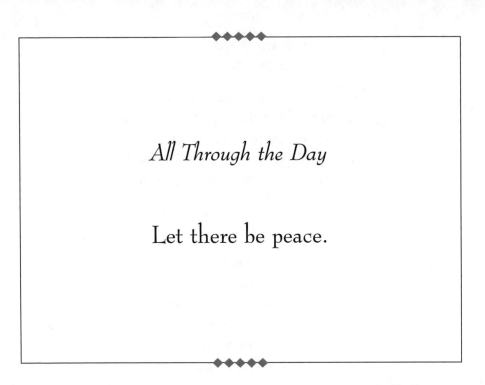

All Through the Day

Let there be peace.

My Day Is Ending

Here in the night,
as my day ends,
I need you
to remind me
that peace has to be learned.

It does not come easily or naturally
to the human heart.

Certainly not to my heart.

Peace is something that
I must learn to love,

and achieve,
whatever the cost.

Like Francis,
I am called not only to be at peace,
but to be a peacemaker,
an instrument of your peace.

No matter what the effort,
no matter what suffering it may require,
I am called, like Francis,
to preserve peace of spirit and body,
out of love of our Lord Jesus Christ.

Day Twenty-Two

My Day Begins

It is easy for us
to define the peace we seek
as the absence of conflict.
But that is not God's peace.
His peace is not
the absence of anything.

It is his presence.

It is his reply
to that hunger of our soul

that only he can satisfy.
It is his response
to the yearning and desire for him
that shapes our lives,
that pulls at the very heart of our being.

Peace is not tranquillity.
It is the ache of a dissatisfied soul.

Peace is
God's gift of himself.

Peace is God
come alive in our soul,
come alive
in every corner of
our day and night.

Peace
is what Francis celebrated
on that day when his soul,
for the first time in his young life,
shook itself free
of everything
but God.

In that moment
Francis redefined peace,
making it, for all of us,
the inescapable support
of our spiritual journey,
the object of
all our yearning,
of all our desire.

All Through the Day

Come alive in my soul.

My Day Is Ending

Here in the night,
as my day ends,
I need you
to remind me
that peace has to be learned.

I need you to teach me.

Your peace
is what my soul
yearns for
and desires.
It is a gift
that only you can give.

So here in the dark
I beg you
once more
to satisfy my soul's hunger
and fill these silent final hours
of the day
with your presence,
with your peace,
with what my soul so deeply desires,
and only you can give.

As another day ends,
teach me.

Day Twenty-Three

■

My Day Begins

*"He desired to possess wisdom
which is better than gold
and to acquire understanding
which is more precious than silver."*

—THOMAS OF CELANO

Francis and those who have
walked in his steps over the centuries
share a common life-changing conviction:

God's peace
is the center of their lives.

It is not
just another pious thought,
whispered along the way.

God's peace,
Francis tells us,
is the point of our lives,
is at the center of our being,
is the goal of our journey.

Knowing this,
spirituality has never been
the same.

Our lives
have never been the same.

Walking in his steps
we have come
to think differently.
Walking in his steps
the world has come
to act differently.

Francis, we have discovered,
is not just another
very holy person
with special spiritual charms.

He is instead
an unlikely spiritual revolutionary,
who changed our lives
by changing our spiritual center.

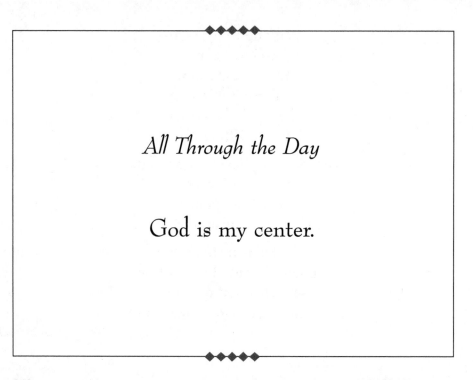

All Through the Day

God is my center.

My Day Is Ending

Here in the night,
as my day ends,
I need you
to remind me
that peace has to be learned.

I need you
to teach my heart
with your gift of peace,
with a wisdom
that is better than gold,
more precious than silver.

I need nothing less
than to change the way I think,
to change the way I live
by changing my center of being.

I need to walk in your footsteps

I need you
to be the center of my soul,
the center of my days,
and the silence of my nights.

I need you now
by my side
as I enter into this night.

As I go where you wait for me.

Day Twenty-Four

My Day Begins

In a quiet unassuming phrase
Angela Foligno,
one of those who followed
in the footsteps of Francis,
spelled out the powerful grounds
for building our lives
on the peace of God:

"My sweet Lord," she prayed,
"who can separate me from you?"

In Angela's simple words, however,
there is a spiritual confidence,
a spiritual courage,
a rock bottom truth
that is at odds with the timidity
that colors so much of our spiritual journey.

With these few words
she reminds us that
the firm ground for our God-centered life
is our conviction that nothing,
absolutely nothing,
can separate us from the Lord.

The irony is that, knowing this,
so many of us
still go tiptoeing
around the God who loves us,
who gives shape to our lives,
as though God were standing guard
at every gateway to our life,
determined to expose our weakness,
as though God's love for us
were as fragile as our faith,
unable to withstand
even the slightest demonstration
of our humanity.

All Through the Day

Nothing can separate me from the Lord.

My Day Is Ending

Here in the night,
as my day ends,
I need you
to remind me
that peace has to be learned.

It does not come easily or naturally
to the human heart.

As this night falls
I need you to gather together
at the center of my soul
the hopes and disappointments
of this day.

But above all
I will need the spiritual courage
that you bring with you.

I need you to remind me,
as this night begins,
that nothing,
absolutely nothing, can separate me
from you, my Lord.

I need to know that you
will stay with me
through the silent darkness of this night,
and that you will be there
when tomorrow comes.

Day Twenty-Five

My Day Begins

It was said about Francis
that he felt he belonged
to one and the same family
with all other creatures.

In everything beautiful
he saw beauty itself.

It was a vision of creation
that never descended into
a vaporous romanticism.

He had a vision of spirituality
that never lost its roots in God's earth.

But most of all
in everything beautiful
he saw beauty itself.

In everything beautiful
he saw God.

In everything beautiful
he saw his family.

It is not like that for us.
We find ourselves
speaking sweetly of our brother the land,
and our sister the pond,
but for us
it is a relationship

that never gets beyond
poetic imagery.

It seldom becomes for us
what it must become,
what it became for Francis
—what it was for Francis—
a call to a demanding family life,
an ongoing commitment
to our brothers and sisters,
to the land, the sky, and the sea.

For Francis
there are no distinctions.
We are all one earth,
we are all one family.

There is only one peace.

All Through the Day

There is only one peace.

My Day Is Ending

Here in the night,
as my day ends,
I need you
to remind me
that peace has to be learned.

It does not come easily or naturally
to the human heart,
certainly not to my heart.

As my day ends,
here in the dark silence of this night,
I need you to surround me,
with the family

that you have given me,
the family that is now mine.

Here in the darkness,
open my eyes
to the beauty of this world.
Let me see the beauty
Francis saw so clearly.

Let me see into
the beauty of this night
and its darkness.

Let me see
as he would see.
Let me see
the beauty in everything.

Day Twenty-Six

My Day Begins

Clare of Assisi,
walking securely, joyfully, and swiftly
in the steps of Francis,
defined for us
what it means
to live God's peace.

For her,
as it can and should be
for us,
peace of soul
means opening our hearts,

leaving them naked and vulnerable,
exposing them to everything
and everyone around them.

It is to recognize
and accept
that peace of soul
is never enjoyed alone.
It always involves
inviting others into our hearts.

The peace of God,
as we come to accept
and treasure,
can never be a synonym
for being untroubled
and unchallenged.

It is not quietude,
not easy-to-come-by serenity.

It is not
living oblivious and insensitive
to the pains of the world around us.

It is rather
a matter of
making room in our soul for
God's children.
All of them.

However uncomfortable
they may make us,
however deeply
they may challenge and change
our definition of peace,
God's definition
of his peace
stands.

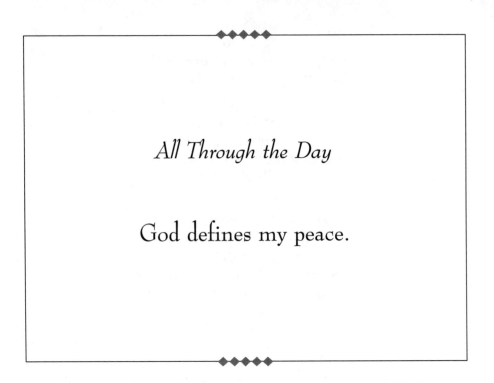

All Through the Day

God defines my peace.

My Day Is Ending

Here in the night,
as another day ends,
I need you
to remind me
that your peace has to be learned.

It does not come easily or naturally
to the human heart,
certainly not to my crowded and busy heart.

As this day ends
I need to rediscover
your gift of peace,
as it can and should be for us.

Keep my heart open.
Make room in my cluttered soul
for all your children,
especially for my brothers and sisters
for whom I have been too busy this day.

Above all,
let me make room for peace.

Let me make sure that
I have left room for you.

Day Twenty-Seven

My Day Begins

Francis of Assisi was
that rarest of saints,
that rarest of men:
a truly happy man,
a truly joyful man,
who, even as he prayed,
was given to singing
and dancing in the streets.

For him one was the other.

He had a sense of joy,
of playfulness,
that permeated and colored
his whole way of life.

He was someone
who was truly
glad in the Lord.

His happiness
set a tone for a lifetime,
his lifetime,
and the lifetimes of thousands
who have chosen
to walk in his steps.

For our lifetimes.

His legacy to us is his sense of joy,
his sense of playfulness
that permeates and colors his whole spirituality,
and given a chance,
ours.

It is a spirituality based
on the happiness of Francis,
not just an occasional happy moment,
but a joy that spreads through every corner
of the life Francis lived in God.

This life can be ours.
It is to walk in his footsteps.
It is to walk in joy.

It is to walk in peace.
It is God calling us to the dance.

All Through the Day

Come to the dance.

My Day Is Ending

Here in the night,
as another day ends,
I need you
to remind me
that your peace
has to be learned,
that to walk in your footsteps
is to walk in joy.

I beg of you
to light up the darkness
of this night
with a joy
that only you can give.

Let it spread
into every corner
of my day and night.

Let it permeate and color
my world.

Replace the darkness
with your sense of joy
and playfulness.

Let your presence be
not just an occasional happy moment,
but the very air
my soul breathes.

Day Twenty-Eight

My Day Begins

In one more attempt
to capture the joy of his presence
and his impact on the world
into which he was born
and which he shaped,
it was said of Francis
that he was
"resplendent as the dawn
and the morning star."

But however great our words,
they fail.
They always do.

The simple truth is that Francis of Assisi
shaped and changed our spiritual world
for the better
and forever.

He did it simply.
He did it by becoming a man of peace.
He came into a world of darkness and cold
and set it afire
with truth and charity.

Francis
brought warmth to the coldness
and light to the darkness.
That's all.

Not much.

But it was and still is,
given a chance,
enough to change our lives
and our world.

His simplicity was
and still is
a spiritual revolution.

He belongs to everybody.

We reach out to him
not because he will make our life easier,
but because in our heart of hearts
we recognize the truth of his life,
and the possibilities of our own.

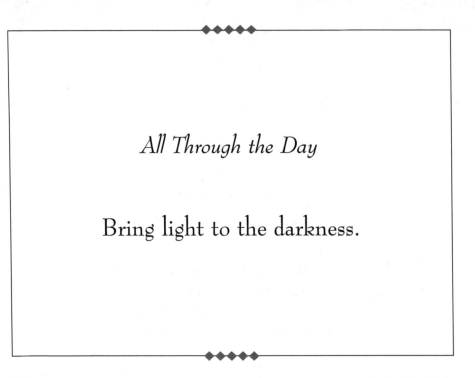

All Through the Day

Bring light to the darkness.

My Day Is Ending

Here in the night,
as another day ends,
I need you
to remind me
that your peace
has to be learned,
and that it can be learned.

Like you,
I can change my life.
I can change the world
by embracing peace.

Here in this night,
with your voice in my heart,
I can believe that all is possible.

The darkness and cold of this night
can be set afire.

With you
I can shape and change
the world I live in.

Here in the night
everything is possible
for those who believe.

I can become a person of peace.

Day Twenty-Nine

My Day Begins

For many of us
life is and has been
an anxiety-driven pursuit of God.

Francis knew it could and should be different.

He knew that life would have to be
turned upside down.

We would have to
change our notion of love
because the peace of God
as lived by Francis

cannot take root in our lives
until we accept the simple
life-overturning truth
that God loves us,
that God waits patiently
for an opportunity to embrace us.

That is different.

Until now
when we have talked about God's love,
it has remained pretty much
something we earn,
something we can lose,
something that in the long run
is pretty much
a reward for being good.

None of this is true.

Spirituality is
the opposite of proving to God
that we are good.
It has nothing to do
with proving anything.

It is accepting and embracing
the extraordinary truth
that we are loved by a God
who only wants to embrace us.

The one who is so good
and so great
desires your embraces
and is waiting to embrace you.

Can we deal with it?
Will we let it happen?

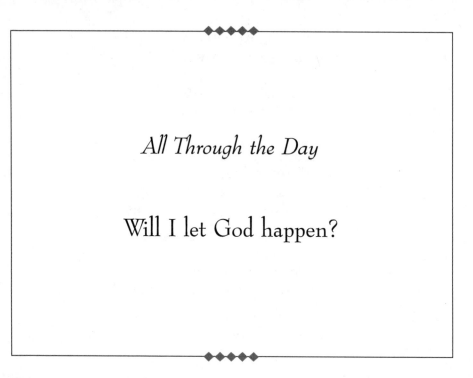

All Through the Day

Will I let God happen?

My Day Is Ending

Here in the night,
as another day ends,
I need you
to remind me
that your peace
has to be learned,
but not your love.

Your love is a pure and endless gift.

It is not mine to earn.
Nor is it something
I could lose.

Your love is here to stay.

I do not have to prove myself.
All I have to do
is accept and embrace
the extraordinary truth

that you love us,
that you love me.
More than anything
you ask of us only
to accept your embrace
and return it.

Let me get out of your way.

Day Thirty

My Day Begins

Francis faced life
with a simple prayer.

In all his preaching,
even before he set forth the word of God,
Francis would first pray
for all those gathered around.

We do the same.
We pray for peace.

Without God's peace in our hearts
the word of God goes unheard.

Without God's peace in our heart
the word of God cannot take root,
cannot grow.

As Francis showed us,
it is only with our hearts at peace
that we can we hear and live
the word of God.

We need to pray
knowing that the peace of God
is a gift,
but it is a gift that is
ours for the asking.

We need to pray, knowing that many who had lost confidence
of ever knowing peace
have with the help of the Lord
embraced peace,
and have become followers of Francis,
children of peace,
the word of God
alive in their hearts.

The word of God
alive in our hearts.

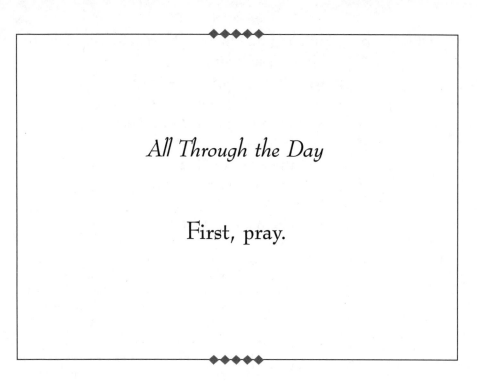

All Through the Day

First, pray.

My Day Is Ending

Here in the night,
as another day ends,
I need you
to remind me
that your peace
has to be learned,
but not your love.

I need you
to teach me
how to pray with confidence.
With your help,
but only with your help,
can I walk in your footsteps.

Only with your help
can I become
a child of peace,
your word alive in my heart.

In any world, at any time,
but especially now,
it seems that peace is hard to come by.

I have lost confidence
in ever knowing peace.

Here in this night
I pray,
share your confidence with me.

One Final Word

This book is meant only to be a gateway to the spiritual wisdom of those who have followed in the footsteps of Francis of Assisi, a gateway that may open doors for your own spiritual path.

You may decide that the way of Francis is not your way. But there are many other teachers, many other traditions. Somewhere there is the right teacher for you, for your own, very special, absolutely unique journey. You will find your teacher; you will discover your path. We would not be searching, as St. Augustine reminds us, if we had not already been found.

One more thing should be said.

Spirituality is not meant to be self-absorption, a cocoonish relationship of God and me. In the long run, if it is to have meaning, if it is to grow and not wither, it must be a wellspring of compassionate living. It must reach out to others as God has reached out to us.

We have to break down the walls of our souls and let in not just heaven, but the whole world. True spirituality reaches out to all the children of God. It does not end in our own consolation but in that all embracing love of others that we call compassion.

You May Also Want to Read

Peace of Heart: Based on the Life and Teachings of Francis of Assisi by John Kirvan, a complementary book that is part of the Thirty Days series.

Books about St. Clare or St. Bonaventure that are part of The Classics of Western Spirituality (Paulist Press).

The Passionate Troubadour: A Medieval Novel About Francis of Assisi by Edward Hays (Forest of Peace Books, 2004).